S0-BZF-130

ABORTION

Pro-Life by Conviction,
Pro-Choice by Default

by

RICHARD EXLEY

Tulsa, Oklahoma

Unless otherwise indicated,
all Scripture quotations are taken from
The Holy Bible: New International Version,
copyright © 1973, 1978, 1984 by the International
Bible Society. Used by permission of Zondervan
Bible Publishers.

*ABORTION — Pro-Life by Conviction,
Pro-Choice by Default*
ISBN 0-89274-673-4
Copyright © 1989 by Richard Exley
7807 E. 76th St.
Tulsa, Oklahoma 74133-3648

Published by Honor Books
P.O. Box 55388
Tulsa, Oklahoma 74155

Printed in the United States of America. All rights
reserved under International Copyright Law. Contents
and/or cover may not be reproduced in whole or in part in
any form without the express written consent of the
Publisher.

DEDICATION

To Mark and Jennifer Crow, whose lives and faithful witness helped to open my eyes to the plight of the unborn.

CONTENTS

PUBLISHER'S STATEMENT

Having been silent for too long on this matter, Honor Books issues this statement of position on the abortion holocaust. Christians can no longer be silent and allow babies to be murdered — the killing must stop. For, as the title of this book suggests, we were pro-life by conviction, but pro-choice by default. Every day more than 4,000 children die from abortion — more than 25 million since the infamous *Roe v. Wade* decision in 1973.

Richard Exley has researched 2,000 pages of material and condensed it into practical terms for the average Christian. You may find the material shocking, but we hope that it grieves you and forces you into action to stop this "choice" they call abortion. As our contribution to the pro-life effort, we have printed this handbook on our nation's greatest crime — abortion.

INTRODUCTION

Abortion is the most critical issue now facing the American church. It is not the only issue, but it is the most critical. Every day, in abortion clinics and hospitals across our nation, four to five thousand pre-born babies are systematically put to death. The total number of casualties, in this war on the pre-born, has now reached more than twenty-five million, and our great land is stained with their innocent blood. If the Church does not arouse herself, both to intercede and to intervene, we will enter a new dark age, a post-Christian era, not unlike that which now envelops the continent of Europe.

Abortion continues largely unchecked because the Church does not grasp the true magnitude of its horror. I am convinced that if Christians fully understood the extent of the abortion holocaust, they would use their considerable power and influence to end the killing. Tragically, the majority of believers simply have little or no understanding of the issue. They have been effectively distanced from the harsh realities of abortion; therefore, they are unaware of what it portends, both for the Church and the nation.

There is a wealth of excellent material on the subject, but most Christians simply have not availed themselves of these resources. Therefore, I have put together a small volume which, although not comprehensive, does address the major issues in a concise manner. It is a handbook which, I hope, will serve as a practical resource for the concerned believer who is hard pressed to find the time to research the subject in depth.

I am especially indebted to those persons who have contributed so much to the pro-life movement. In particular I would like to thank Dr. Bernard Nathanson, John Powell, S.J., and Mark Belz for the invaluable contributions they have made through their writings on the subject.

Finally, I have written from the assumption that most people who will read this book are already convinced of the scriptural teachings in regard to the beginning of life and its sanctity. Consequently, rather than presenting a biblical exegesis on the subject, I have attempted to address some of the more common arguments raised by the pro-choice advocates. In no way should this approach be construed as an effort to minimize the importance of the Scriptures. In truth, all of the convictions contained herein are deeply rooted in the Judeo-Christian ethic which is firmly based on the Bible.

"When he opened the fifth seal, I saw under the altar the souls of those who had been slain. . . .They called out in a loud voice, 'How long, Sovereign Lord, holy and true, until you judge the inhabitants of the earth and avenge our blood?' "

Revelation 6:9,10

Chapter 1

AMERICA'S DARKEST DAY

Consider with me, if you will, the darkest day in American history.

I am not referring to the winter that General Washington and the Continental Army spent at Valley Forge, though by all accounts it was a torturous time. Historians tell us: "In the entire dwindling army of eleven thousand men, there may have been less than a dozen properly equipped for the terrible winter.

". . . As the winter wore on, life at Valley Forge became an unbearable nightmare. Now there were men who were literally naked, because they did not have even rags to wrap around them. . . . And disease was taking a fearful toll of their numbers; they would lose one in four to flu, smallpox, typhus, and exposure."[1]

Nor am I referring to the Civil War when more than five hundred thousand men lost their lives in a terrible conflict which divided the nation and pitted brother against brother, friend against friend.

Neither am I referring to the stock market crash of 1929, nor the Great Depression which followed, with its soup kitchens, bread lines and dust storms. I am not even thinking of the tragedy of December 7, 1941, when the Japanese staged a sneak attack on the United States naval base at Pearl Harbor, inflicting on America one of her most costly defeats. Nor am I speaking of that fateful Thursday afternoon in Dallas, Texas, when a sniper's bullet struck down President John F. Kennedy, and with him the hopes and dreams of an entire generation.

No, I am not referring to the My Lai massacre of March 16, 1968, when the First Platoon of "Charlie" Company, under the command of Lieutenant William L. Calley, Jr., participated in the wholesale slaughter of between five hundred and six hundred unarmed Vietnamese villagers. I am not even talking about the Watergate scandal, which destroyed the last remnant of trust that post-Vietnam Americans had in the integrity of their government.

No, as dark as those days were, they pale in comparison to that fateful day — Monday, January 22, 1973 — when the United States Supreme Court ruled 7-2, in the now famous *Roe v. Wade* decision, which declared unconstitutional a Texas law preventing abortion except to save the life of the mother. That ruling struck down all existing laws forbidding abortion, and gave the United States the dubious distinction of having the most permissive abortion laws of any nation in the western hemisphere.

With that decision, the United States Supreme Court denied an untold number of persons their most fundamental right — the inalienable right to life! To date, twenty-five million unborn babies have perished as a result, and only

2

God knows how many more will die before we put an end to this evil holocaust.

Endnote

1. Peter Marshall and David Manuel, *The Light and the Glory* (Old Tappan, New Jersey: Fleming H. Revell, 1977), pp. 320-322.

Chapter 2

THE WAR ON THE UNBORN

In the early 1980s the military government in Argentina conducted what was known as "The Dirty War." Political opponents, personal enemies and suspected "insurrectionists" were arrested and carried away in the middle of the night, never to be seen again. With wanton disregard for their human rights, thousands were executed in this political purge. The United States condemned these brutalities, while sanctioning a far more comprehensive and reprehensible "dirty war" of her own.

I'm talking about abortion — the war on the unborn which is being conducted behind the closed doors of clinics and hospitals across America. The number of casualties is absolutely mind-boggling: between four thousand and five thousand every day; twenty-five million in the last sixteen years!

Most of us have difficulty putting numbers of that magnitude into perspective, so let me see if I can help. If we were to execute twenty-five million Americans, it would wipe out the equivalent of the entire population of the states of Washington, Oregon, Nevada, Idaho, Montana, Wyoming, Utah, Arizona, Colorado, New Mexico, North Dakota, South Dakota, Nebraska, Kansas and half of Oklahoma. In reality that's what we have done. In sixteen short years America has killed twenty-five million unborn babies — a number equivalent to the total population of fourteen and one-half states!

You may still be having difficulty grasping the magnitude of the abortion atrocity, so let me try again to illustrate its gigantic proportions. During her 213-year history, the United States has fought six major wars, in which the total casualties numbered 1,296,081.[1] In this sixteen-year war on the unborn, we have suffered almost twenty times that many casualties.

Think of it: in six major wars and 213 years of history we have sustained a total of 1.3 million casualties, while in sixteen short years since that fateful Supreme Court decision we have killed more than twenty-five million unborn babies!

Indulge me one last time: in a single year we suffer approximately two hundred thousand more casualties in this war on the unborn than the United States has sustained in all the wars of her 213-year history.

One can only lament the tragic waste of human potential, not to mention the unconscionable and inconsolable loss of innocent lives.

With its recent decision in the *Webster v. Missouri* case, the United States Supreme Court has given us a chance to end this terrible holocaust. We can put a stop to abortions on demand and see that the unborn are guaranteed their constitutional right to life!

I, for one, agree with Thomas Jefferson, who wrote: "We hold these truths to be self-evident, that all men are created equal, that they are endowed by their Creator with certain unalienable Rights, that among these are Life, Liberty, and the pursuit of Happiness."[2]

Endnotes

1. John Powell, S.J., *Abortion: The Silent Holocaust* (Valencia, California: Tabor Publishing Company, a division of DLM, Inc., 1981).

2. Nelson Manfred Blake, *A Short History of American Life* (New York: McGraw-Hill Book Company, Inc., 1952), p. 130.

Chapter 3

A POIGNANT WITNESS

Do you know what Bernard Nathanson, Anthony Levatino, Joseph Randall, Debra Henry, and Carol Everett have in common?

Probably not, so let me tell you. Nathanson, Levatino and Randall are all doctors with more than one hundred thousand abortions to their combined credit. Debra Henry is a certified medical assistant who worked for six months in a Detroit area abortion clinic. And Carol Everett was the director of two Dallas area abortion clinics from 1977 until 1983. "Was" is the key word here. Now they are all part of an increasing number of professionals who are deserting the abortion industry.

Dr. Bernard Nathanson, a founder of the abortion movement, was the first to renounce his involvement. Today he is an eloquent exponent of the unborn. He is best known for his narration of "The Silent Scream," a documentary film which uses ultrasonic real-time scanning to show what happens to the baby during an abortion.

Dr. Anthony Levatino performed abortions for eight years, but was always vaguely troubled by it. And well he might have been. He performed dilatation and evacuation in late-term abortions, which means that he was literally ". . . pulling out pieces of unborn children."[1]

It took a personal tragedy to finally enable him to give up his lucrative abortion practice. His young daughter was fatally injured when she was hit by an auto in front of the family home. She died in Levatino's arms.

" 'If you lose a child, you look at things differently,' he said. 'What was once uncomfortable becomes intolerable. You feel that you're destroying a human being for money, like a paid assassin.' "[2]

Dr. Joseph Randall, who was an Atlanta clinic operator, estimates that he performed thirty-two thousand abortions. He says, "(After the operation) you have to reassemble that baby — arms, legs, head, chest — everything (to be sure no pieces remain in the mother). That's when it got rough, even for old-timers like me."[3]

He finally stopped performing these operations after a Christian woman convinced him of the immorality of abortion. Today he does volunteer counseling at a facility offering alternatives to abortion.

For Debra Henry, who assisted during abortions, the worst part was hearing the baby's bones breaking as the doctor was taking it out of its mother. She quit after an encounter with a right-to-lifer who was picketing the clinic. Today she is assistant director of the Michigan Pro-Life Action League.

Carol Everett knows about the trauma of abortion first hand. She had an abortion which precipitated an emotional crisis that resulted in a painful divorce. Later she became involved as a merchant of death, operating two clinics in the Dallas area.

Although she was earning a sizeable income and was considered "successful," she became consumed by guilt. She simply could not deny the ever-present evidence that abortion was the killing of a baby. Additionally she was troubled by the gross malpractice which was occurring at the expense of women who had been led to believe that there was little or no risk involved. Eventually she sold her highly profitable business, contributing most of the proceeds to the right-to-life movement, which she continues to support by maintaining a heavy speaking schedule.

These one-time proponents of abortion are now its most active adversaries. Surely their poignant witness cannot be ignored.

Endnotes

1. Don Feder, "Sick of Death," *The Pentecostal Evangel*, Nov. 27, 1988, p. 12. Used by permission of Heritage Features Syndicate.

2. Ibid.

3. Ibid.

Chapter 4

A WOMAN'S RIGHT?

No issue since the slavery question has generated as much polarity as has abortion. Even the United States Supreme Court, that august body of judicial dignitaries, is severely divided on this question. Although the members of the highest court in the land traditionally place a premium on unity, they issued five separate opinions in the 1989 decision of *Webster v. Reproductive Health Services*. And the language of these opinions was divisive.

Justice Harry Blackmun, author of the 1973 *Roe v. Wade* ruling, called the Webster decision "very ominous" and said, ". . . (it) casts into darkness the hopes and visions of every woman in the country who had come to believe that the Constitution guaranteed her the right to exercise some control over her unique ability to bear children." He concluded: "A chill wind blows."

Reactions from others outside the court who are involved in the issue are just as diverse and contradictory.

Randle Terry, founder of Operation Rescue,* a pro-life group which utilizes nonviolent intervention to block abortion clinic doors, thus preventing the killing of unborn babies, said on national television that the idea that the founding fathers intended the Constitution to guarantee a woman the right to kill her unborn baby is ludicrous.

Molly Yard, president of NOW (National Organization for Women), declared war on all those "no-nothings" in government, including President George Bush, who oppose abortion on demand. "We are going to turn this country upside down," she declared, "because we are not going to take it any more."

In the same vein, a spokeswoman for the National Abortion Rights Action League issued a warning to state and national politicians: "Read our lips. Take our freedom, lose your job."

It should be readily obvious that the opposing sides approach the abortion question from different perspectives. The pro-abortion advocates contend that it is a woman's right to control her reproductive life. They claim that the decision to have an abortion is a "personal choice" protected by the Constitution under the right of privacy. Pro-life forces, on the other hand, focus on the rights of the unborn baby. Pointing to both the Declaration of Independence and the Fifth and Fourteenth Amendments to the Constitution, they claim that the unborn have an inalienable right to life.

In considering these issues, it is interesting to note that all of the scientific advances of the past sixteen years, which

---

*For a brief explanation of Operation Rescue, please see Chapter 29.

now prove conclusively that life begins at conception, have been largely ignored by the pro-abortion forces. If anything, their demands for unrestricted abortions have grown more militant. While now admitting that "it" (the fetus) is alive, they continue to adamantly refuse to acknowledge that the unborn child is a person with constitutional rights, including the right to life.

Their position shouldn't really be surprising considering the faulty logic of the *Roe v. Wade* decision. The writer of the majority opinion declared: "We need not resolve the difficult question of when life begins. When those trained in the respective disciplines of medicine, philosophy and theology are unable to arrive at any consensus, the judiciary, at this point in the development of man's knowledge, is not in a position to speculate as to the answer."[1]

We can only conclude that what Justice Blackmun was really saying is, "As long as there is the slightest doubt as to when life begins, the court is not going to provide the unborn any constitutional protection."

Such a conclusion demonstrates a frightening indifference to the sanctity of life. If there is any question as to whether the fetus is a living entity, then it should be protected by the court. To do otherwise is, as history has proven, to set in motion forces which show a blatant disregard for the increasing scientific evidence proving the existence of life from conception.

Germain Grisez, the Catholic philosopher, put it succinctly when he said: "To be willing to kill what for all we know could be a person is to be willing to kill if it is a person."[2]

This tragic truth was driven home to me some time ago while watching a television news special. A woman who was scheduled for an abortion said of her unborn baby, "It's alive, but it's not a person." A doctor at an abortion clinic went a step further. Not only did he acknowledge that "it" was alive, but he also admitted that "it" had rights. He concluded: "Someone's rights have to take precedence over another's. I have no difficulty in choosing maternal rights over fetal rights."[3]

Are the unborn alive? Without a doubt! Do they have the same inherent rights as a person already born? Of course. And, in the light of that truth, I can only concur with Dr. Bernard N. Nathanson who said, "We must courageously face the fact — finally — that human life of a special order is being taken....Denial of this reality is the crassest kind of moral evasiveness."[4]

Endnotes

1. Justice Harry Blackmun, "Roe v. Wade," quoted in Aborting America by Bernard N. Nathanson, M.D., with Richard N. Ostling (Garden City, N.Y.: Doubleday and Company, 1979), p. 207.

2. Ibid., p. 260.

3. Quoted on "48 Hours," Columbia Broadcasting Corporation, June 22, 1989.

4. Nathanson, p. 165.

Chapter 5

WHEN DOES LIFE BEGIN?

The Supreme Court concluded, in its 1973 *Roe v. Wade* decision, that there was not enough evidence to determine when life begins; therefore, the unborn were denied their constitutional right to life. In response one medical school professor, Dr. Eugene Diamond, said, " 'Either the justices were fed a backwoods biology or they were pretending ignorance about a scientific certainty.' "[1]

I can only conclude that they were pretending ignorance. In the early days of the abortion debate, long before the Supreme Court decision, an editorial on the New Ethic which appeared in *California Medicine* stated: " 'There is a curious avoidance of the scientific fact, which everyone really knows, that human life begins at conception.' "[2]

This avoidance continues even now, in the face of ever-mounting evidence concerning life in the womb. Consider, for instance, the hearings which the U.S. Congress held on April 23 and 24, 1981. A group of internationally known geneticists appeared before a Senate judiciary subcommittee to address the question of when human life begins. With one exception they all declared that human life begins at the moment of conception.

Dr. Jerome LeJeune, professor of fundamental genetics at the University of Descarte, Paris, France, testified:

" 'Life has a very, very long history, but each individual has a very neat beginning, *the moment of its conception.*' "[3] (emphasis mine)

Dr. Micheline Matthews-Roth, principal research associate of the Harvard University Medical School, said:

" 'In biology and in medicine, it is an accepted fact that the life of any individual organism reproducing by sexual reproduction begins at conception...therefore it is scientifically correct to say that an individual human life begins at conception, when the egg and sperm join to form the zygote, *and that this developing human always is a member of our species in all stages of its life.*' "[4] (emphasis mine)

Professor Hymie Gordon, chairman of the Department of Medical Genetics at the Mayo Clinic, says:

" 'By all the criteria of modern molecular biology, life is present from the moment of conception.' "[5]

There were several others, including Dr. McCarthy DeMere, attorney, practicing physician and professor of law at the University of Tennessee; Dr. Alfred Bongiovanni, formerly chairman of pediatrics at the University of Ife in Nigeria and currently a member of the faculty of the University of Pennsylvania Medical School; Dr. Jasper Williams, past president of the National Medical

Association; and Dr. Watson A. Bowes, Jr., of the University of Colorado Medical School. Without exception they testified that life begins at conception.[6]

Thanks to the development of the science of fetology, we are now able to study the human fetus. And, according to Dr. Bernard Nathanson, "All of those studies have concluded without exception that the unborn child is a human being, indistinguishable from any of us and an integral part of our human community."[7]

Consider these facts concerning the development of the living human fetus:

By the third week of pregnancy: "The embryo has a primitive pulsating heart and a system of blood vessels. It is manufacturing its own blood, independently of the mother and often of a different type from hers. The brain, liver, pancreas, lungs, spinal cord, and nerve system are forming."[8]

By the fifth week: "All major structures of the body are in evidence, and important muscle groups are in place."[9]

By the sixth week: "The four chambers of the heart are complete, and the heartbeat is very much like it will be in adult life. The child has detectable brain waves."[10]

By the twelfth week: "All organ systems are complete and functioning. Digestive system is complete. Bone marrow is producing blood. The part of the brain associated with pain perception (the thalamus) and the nervous system are well developed."[11]

Yet, as impressive and irrefutable as this evidence is, let us remember that this is just the beginning. "Our capacity to measure signs of life is daily becoming more sophisticated, and as time goes by, we will doubtless be able to isolate life signs at earlier and earlier stages in fetal development."[12]

Given this information, we can no longer pretend that abortion is the sole right of the woman. To do so constitutes either a conspiracy against the pre-born or a willful negligence.

Endnotes

1. John Powell, S.J., *Abortion: The Silent Holocaust* (Valencia, California: Tabor Publishing Company, a division of DLM, Inc., 1981), pp. 68, 69.

2. Ibid., p. 69.

3. Ibid, p. 70.

4. Ibid., pp. 70, 71.

5. Ibid., p. 71.

6. Ibid., pp. 72-74.

7. Donald S. Smith, Don Tanner, ed., *The Silent Scream* (Anaheim, California: American Portrait Films Books, 1985), p. 74.

8. Ibid.

9. Ibid.

10. Ibid.

11. Ibid. p. 75.

12. Bernard N. Nathanson, M.D., with Richard N. Ostling, *Aborting America* (Garden City, New York: Doubleday and Company, 1979), pp. 164, 165.

Chapter 6

MOTHER AND CHILD

Those who favor abortion on demand would have us believe that it is simply a matter of women's rights. They claim that a woman can never be truly free until she has absolute control over her reproductive life. Wrap that argument in euphemistic language like "freedom of choice," or "a woman's constitutional right to privacy," and you can make a pretty good case for legalized abortion. Unfortunately, it ignores several vital factors, including the rights of the unborn.

The unborn child, whether we call it an embryo or a fetus, is not a part of the woman's body like an organ. Dr. Albert W. Liley, a world-renowned research professor in perinatal physiology at the National Women's Hospital in Auckland, New Zealand, writes:

" 'Biologically, at no stage can we subscribe to the view that the fetus is merely an appendage of the mother. Genetically, mother and baby are separate individuals from conception.' "[1]

Dr. Daniel Callahan, director of the Institute of Society, Ethics and the Life Sciences, concurs:

"Genetically, hormonally and in all organic respects save the source of its nourishment, a fetus and even an embryo is separate from the woman."[2]

Dr. Bernard Nathanson, one of the founding fathers of the National Abortion Rights Action League, now argues eloquently for the rights of the unborn. On the question of a woman's rights over her own body, he says:

"Leaving aside for the moment the question of whether (the fetus) is merely 'part' of the mother's body like an appendix, this principle is wrongheaded in any event. Civilized societies do not permit women absolute control over their bodies; they do not sanction such things as mutilation of one's own body, drug abuse, prostitution, or suicide. Even if (the fetus) is to be considered merely a woman's 'property' and not the 'person' that the anti-abortionists claim, control over property is not absolute — statutes against cruelty to animals are legitimate, including the animals that the violator owns.

"...In the contemporary situation, the woman's 'control over her body' offers her a number of options other than abortion. She can choose sexual continence, or if not continence, then contraception, or if not contraception, then sterilization, or if none of these, she can take control in making sure that the man in her life makes such a choice."[3]

In short, abortion is not simply a question of women's rights, and even if it were, there is a moral and legal precedent for balancing individual rights with the rights of others. For instance, my right to swing my fist stops just short of your face.

Endnotes

1. John Powell, S.J., *Abortion: The Silent Holocaust* (Valencia, California: Tabor Publishing Company, a division of DLM, Inc., 1981), p. 115.

2. Bernard N. Nathanson, M.D., with Richard N. Ostling, *Aborting America* (Garden City, New York: Doubleday and Company, 1979), pp. 203, 204.

3. Ibid., pp. 191, 192.

Chapter 7

LEGAL SCHIZOPHRENIA

It has been said that when a government passes an unjust or immoral law, then the law is at war with itself. Historically, a case in point is the Fugitive Slave Act. As Maria Child argued so persuasively before the Massachusetts legislators:

"Law was established to maintain justice between man and man; and this (law) clearly maintains injustice. Law was instituted to protect the weak from the strong; this (law) delivers the weak completely into the arbitrary power of the strong....That act...commands what is wrong, and forbids what is right....It forbids us to shelter the homeless, to protect abused innocents, to feed the hungry, to 'hide the outcast.' Let theological casuists argue as they will, Christian hearts will shrink from thinking of Jesus as surrendering a fugitive....Political casuists may exercise their skill in making the worse appear the better reason, still all honest minds have an intuitive perception that no human enactment which violates God's laws is worthy of respect...."[1]

Current laws, making abortion on demand legal, bear a frightening affinity with the Fugitive Slave Act. They too make "lawful" what is unlawful — the taking of human life — and forbid as "unlawful" that which is right — the rescue of the unborn child.

These unjust laws also make possible a wide spectrum of events which can only be described as bizarre.

For instance, the killing of the unborn is now defended as a woman's constitutional right to privacy, while the non-violent attempt to rescue the unborn from certain death is called "criminal trespass." Judges find themselves required by law to sentence, as common criminals, conscientious citizens who find it impossible to look the other way while the unborn are being put to death. Law-abiding citizens of moral conscience now find that they must choose between obeying an immoral law, which allows the killing of the unborn, or violate that law in an attempt to save the lives of pre-born babies.

Perhaps the most graphic example of this legal schizophrenia is related by Dr. Ron Bryce in a recent article entitled "The Killing of a 'Nonperson.' " In this account, Dr. Bryce tells of treating a baby which had survived an attempted abortion:

"The situation seemed absurd. Here was a tiny human being who just minutes before had been legally a nonperson. After surviving the abortion attempt, however, he was considered a person and was entitled to his right for adequate care.

"Paradoxically the same medical system that had failed to kill him was now attempting to save his life."[2]

"In a world in which adults control power and purse," writes Dr. Albert W. Liley, "the fetus is at a disadvantage, being small, naked and nameless and voiceless. He has no one except sympathetic adults to speak up for him and defend him — equally no one except callous adults to condemn and attack him."[3]

The only way out of this chaos is a return to laws which maintain justice for all: both the strong and the weak, both the rich and the poor, both the born and the unborn. Until such laws are enacted, Christians have a special responsibility.

We must:

> "Speak up for those who cannot speak
>   for themselves,
> for the rights of all who are
>   destitute.
> Speak up and judge fairly;
> defend the rights of the poor and
>   needy."
>
> Proverbs 31:8,9

We must:

> "Defend the cause of the weak and
>   fatherless;
>   maintain the rights of the poor and
>   oppressed.
> Rescue the weak and needy;
>   deliver them from the hand of the
>   wicked."
>
> Psalm 82:3,4

Endnotes

1. Maria Child, "THE DUTY OF DISOBEDIENCE TO THE FUGITIVE SLAVE ACT: AN APPEAL TO THE LEGISLATORS OF MASSACHUSETTS" (Boston: excerpts from "Anti-Slavery Tract No. 9," published by the American Anti-Slavery Society, 1860), quoted in *SUFFER THE LITTLE CHILDREN* by Mark Belz (Westchester, Illinois: Crossway Books, a division of Good News Publishers, 1989), p. 167.

2. Ron Bryce, M.D., "The Killing of a 'Nonperson,' " *Pentecostal Evangel*, June 11, 1989, p. 19.

3. John Powell, S.J., *Abortion: The Silent Holocaust* (Valencia, California: Tabor Publishing Company, a division of DLM, Inc., 1981), p. 115.

Chapter 8

A DANGEROUS DENIAL

We have reached a frightening point in human history when we can knowingly and dispassionately terminate a human life, as is being done more than four thousand times a day in abortion clinics across America. The "justification" for this wanton slaughter of the unborn is twofold: 1) so-called women's rights, and 2) something referred to as "personhood" (or the lack thereof).

Sixteen years ago, when the United States Supreme Court issued its ruling in the now-famous Roe v. Wade case, there were a lot of questions concerning the exact moment when human life begins. Much ado was made of "viability," or that time when the fetus is ". . . potentially able to live outside the mother's womb albeit with artificial aid."[1]

Thus we ended up with the trimester system, which in essence allowed fully elective abortions for approximately six out of the nine months of a woman's pregnancy.

With its recent Webster ruling, the court let stand a Missouri statute which placed the beginning of life at conception, while retaining the viability concept — although the time of viability was pushed back to twenty weeks. While this is a step in the right direction, it is hardly satisfactory. It acknowledges the fact that the unborn child has life from conception, but it continues to deny his personhood until viability can be proven.

In some ways, this ruling is even more ominous than its predecessors, for it knowingly justifies the taking of innocent life and denies the unborn their constitutional rights on the basis of their "personhood" or the lack thereof. In the Roe decision, personhood was loosely defined. The unborn fetus was considered a person, or at least a potential person, when it ". . . presumably has the capability of meaningful life outside the mother's womb."[2]

The significant word here is "meaningful"; yet it is nowhere defined.

What constitutes personhood or meaningful life? Who is to judge? What makes life "meaningful," and based on what criteria? If we base our decision on the prevailing pro-abortion rhetoric, then the unborn baby is not a person unless it is wanted by the mother — unless it is perfectly healthy, free from any deformity or other abnormality.

The problem with that kind of reasoning is that it is based on the subjective opinion of a biased party — namely, the mother and/or the abortionist. Not only does this approach deny the unborn their constitutional rights, it also opens a Pandora's box of potential abuses.

Mary Anne Warren, a pro-abortion philosopher, says, "A fetus is a human being which is not yet a person."[3] To her way of thinking, biological human life does not constitute personhood, for which she rather proposes five criteria:

1. Consciousness and the 'capacity to feel pain.'

2. Reasoning.

3. Self-motivated activity.

4. Ability to communicate.

5. The presence of self-concepts and self-awareness.[4]

This kind of thinking, be it carefully considered or blandly accepted, denies the inherent sanctity of life and moves us ever closer to infanticide. And not only to infanticide, but to the disposal of the "...comatose adult, the severe psychotic, the retardate with an I.Q. of 25, or the catatonic schizophrenic with an I.Q. of 180."[5] In fact, it opens the way to the potential disposal of anyone who may be judged a non-productive or undesired member of society.

Now, before you conclude that I am some kind of pro-life fanatic, spouting inflammatory rhetoric, let me remind you that highly respected professionals in the fields of medicine and science are already proposing just such things.

For instance, "A Yale University geneticist, Dr. Y. Edward Hsia...suggested mandatory prenatal tests to discover defective unborn babies and in such cases, compulsory death for the defective by abortion."[6]

Then there's the case of Nobel Laureate, Dr. Francis Crick, who was quoted in the Pacific News Service (January 1978) as stating: " 'No newborn infant should be declared human until it has passed certain tests regarding its genetic endowment and that if it fails these tests it forfeits the right to live."[7]

If we continue to permit abortions on demand, in spite of the fact that we now know the unborn are alive, we are jeopardizing our entire way of life. To ignore this reality is to practice denial of the most dangerous kind.

Endnotes

1. "*Roe v. Wade,*" quoted in *Aborting America* by Bernard N. Nathanson, M.D., with Richard N. Ostling (Garden City, New York: Doubleday and Company, 1979), p. 207.

2. Ibid., p. 209.

3. Ibid., p. 222.

4. Ibid., pp. 222, 223.

5. Ibid., p. 225.

6. John Powell, S.J., *Abortion: The Silent Holocaust* (Valencia, California: Tabor Publishing Company, a division of DLM, Inc., 1981), p. 49.

7. Ibid, p. 44.

Chapter 9

THE FATAL FIRST STEP

Most of us would like to think of abortion as a private decision affecting only the mother and her pre-born child. Nothing could be farther from the truth. As Malcolm Muggeridge wrote in an article in the *Human Life Review* (Fall, 1977), the legalization of abortion on demand is a "slippery slope." Once we deprive even a single person (or a select group like the pre-born) of the inalienable right to life, we have taken that "fatal first step" toward death on demand.

In October 1973, just nine months after the Supreme Court decision legalizing abortion, the *New England Journal of Medicine* published a paper by Drs. Raymond S. Duff and A.G.M. Campbell of the Yale University Medical School which openly advocated the option of death for defective infants.

Newsweek magazine (November 12, 1973) quoted Duff: " 'The public has to decide what to do with vegetated individuals who have no human potential.' " Sondra

Diamond of Philadelphia responded with a letter to the editor:

" 'I must confess that I fit the description of a 'vegetable' as defined in the article *Shall This Child Die*?

" 'Due to severe brain damage incurred at birth, I am unable to dress myself, toilet myself, or write; my secretary is typing this letter. Many thousands of dollars had to be spent on my rehabilitation and education in order for me to reach my present professional status as a counseling psychologist. My parents were also told, 35 years ago, that there was 'little or no hope' of achieving meaningful 'humanhood' for their daughter. Have I reached 'humanhood'? Compared with Drs. Duff and Campbell, I believe I have surpassed it!

" 'Instead of changing the law to make it legal to weed out us 'vegetables,' let us change the laws so that we may receive quality medical care, education and freedom to live as full and productive lives as our potentials allow.' "[1]

When we consider the unborn who are found to have severe genetic disorders, the questions surrounding abortion become more complex and infinitely more painful. While such cases represent a number so small as to be statistically insignificant, the issue is unbearably real for those who are personally involved.

"Kate Maloy, a Pittsburgh writer who six years ago had an abortion after learning that the baby she was carrying had a rare and severely damaging genetic disorder, says, 'the decision I had to make involved an intense moral struggle — and one that no judge or legislator would ever have to go through.' She adds: 'To consent to the loss of a wanted baby and be an agent in that loss was dreadful, but the choice was mine. . . . I couldn't subject a child to that kind of suffering.' "[2]

My heart goes out to her, it really does, but I cannot believe that death is the best solution. Although such hard decisions are usually justified by saying that action is being taken in the "best interest" of the unborn child, I think it might be more honest to acknowledge that the real concern is chiefly the supposed burden the child would place upon parents or society.

I agree with former Surgeon-General C. Everett Koop, an internationally known pediatric surgeon, who said; " 'It has been my constant experience that disability and unhappiness do not necessarily go together. Some of the most unhappy children whom I have known have all of their physical and mental faculties, and on the other hand some of the happiest youngsters have borne burdens which I myself would find very difficult to bear. Our obligation in such circumstances is to find alternatives for the problems our patients face. I don't consider death an acceptable alternative. With our technology and creativity, we are merely at the beginning of what we can do educationally and in the field of leisure for such youngsters. And who knows what happiness is for another person?' "[3]

By now it should be readily obvious that abortion is not a private decision, but a public one, affecting not only the pre-born child, but society as we know it. Once we accept death as a viable option under certain conditions, we have opened up ourselves to the unthinkable — death on demand.

Endnotes

1. Sondra Diamond, quoted in *Abortion: The Silent Holocaust* by John Powell, S.J. (Valencia, California: Tabor Publishing Company, a division of DLM, Inc., 1981), pp. 46, 47.

2. Kate Maloy, quoted in *The Wall Street Journal*, July 5, 1989.

3. Bernard N. Nathanson, M.D., with Richard N. Ostling, *Aborting America* (Garden City, New York: Doubleday and Company, 1979), pp. 235, 236.

Chapter 10

IN THE CASE OF RAPE OR INCEST

Many pro-life advocates are pro-choice when it comes to pregnancies resulting from rape or incest. At first glance this viewpoint seems reasonable enough, but upon careful examination we can only conclude that, even in such unfortunate situations, abortion is not the answer.

Clayton Lewis, director of the Biblical Action League, writes: "Pregnancy from rape and incest presents special problems. Those cruel and brutal acts (however) are not mitigated by the perpetration of more brutalities."[1]

In the case of a pregnancy resulting from rape, abortion is simply not a viable solution, for several reasons:

First, it punishes the wrong person — the pre-born child. No civilized system of justice would execute a child because of his father's crimes. The Scriptures declare: "Fathers shall not be put to death for their children, nor children put to death for their fathers; each is to die for his own sin" (Deut. 24:16).

nd, it in no way mitigates the trauma of rape or incest. Quite naturally the victim wants to rid herself of every memory of that violent experience, but an abortion will not accomplish this. Only the healing grace of the Lord Jesus Christ, expressed through the ministry of the Holy Spirit, can make her whole. If anything, an abortion only adds to the woman's shame. Now she is not only the victim of a violent act, but the perpetrator of one as well. Indeed, she has become one with the very thing she most despises.

Third, abortion carries with it certain inherent spiritual and psychological consequences. It is not a benign act; rather it is an act of violence. The woman who has an abortion sins, not only against her baby, but also against herself, and against the laws of God. When a person takes the life of another, a part of the person's self also dies. The person is somehow diminished.

Fourth, abortion is evidence of a failure to trust the grace of God. I do not mean to trivialize the anguish of rape or the complications of a subsequent, unwanted pregnancy, but I do want to emphasize the truth of God's sovereignty and His ability to redeem any situation.

A case in point is the late Ethel Waters. She was conceived as the result of a knife-point rape when her mother was just a child of twelve. Since abortion was illegal, her mother carried her to term, and the world is the better for it. The ministry in song of Ethel Waters has blessed thousands during the Billy Graham evangelistic crusades.

To summarize this chapter, perhaps a cliche from my childhood says it best: "Two wrongs don't make a right!"

Endnote

1. Personal letter.

Chapter 11

ABORTION AND CHILD ABUSE

Almost no one denies that life begins in the womb, early in pregnancy, probably at conception. Yet, pro-abortion advocates still contend that abortion is a woman's right and her private choice!

Such arguments may have been convincing before the invention of ultrasound and the development of the science of fetology. But in the light of what we have learned about the life of the unborn, these contentions can now only be described as shallow and self-serving.

An unplanned pregnancy can create a number of difficulties, especially if the mother is unmarried and/or poor, not to mention still in her teens. I have heard abortion "justified" in such cases on a purely economic basis:

"It's cheaper in the long run for taxpayers to pay for abortions rather than letting unwanted babies be born and become a burden upon society."

Of all the supposed reasons for abortion, I find this one the most dehumanizing. The value of a human life simply cannot be measured in dollars and cents.

Another pro-abortion contention is that to force a mother to give birth to a child she does not want and cannot provide for is to condemn the child to a life of abuse. Such arguments are based on the assumption that an unwanted child will be an abused child. Yet there is no documented sociological or psychological evidence to support this hypothesis. The only real documented factor in child abuse is the fact that its victims often grow up to be abusive parents themselves.

And we might also note that statistics reveal a marked increase in the incidence of child abuse since the *Roe v. Wade* decision sixteen years ago. Although our society has destroyed more than twenty-five million "unwanted" babies, child abuse continues to increase rather than to decrease. I am not categorically stating that there is a direct correlation between legalized abortion and child abuse, but I cannot help but wonder: in truth, is not abortion the ultimate act of child abuse?

Chapter 12

THE RIGHT TO LIFE

Many of those who favor pro-choice say that they personally feel that abortion is wrong, but that they respect the woman's right to decide for herself.

Upon first hearing, this sounds reasonable enough, even American, but upon closer examination one discovers a fatal flaw. Such logic fails to take into account the life of the pre-born child. Any argument, or even any law, that considers only one of the parties involved is fundamentally biased and unsound, and therefore not to be trusted.

Although many pro-life people are evangelical Christians, the debate about abortion is not a religious question. It has nothing to do with freedom of religion, or with the separation of Church and state, as the pro-abortion forces often attempt to argue. It is a human rights issue.

The real question is: Does anyone have the right to arbitrarily take the life of another person?

Now that's a matter of human rights in its most basic form!

In his Personhood Proclamation of January 14, 1988, former President Ronald Reagan declared: "That right to life belongs equally to babies in the womb, babies born handicapped, and the elderly or infirm. That we have killed the unborn for 15 years does not nullify this right, nor could any number of killings ever do so. The unalienable right to life is found not only in the Declaration of Independence but also in the Constitution that every President is sworn to preserve, protect, and defend. Both the Fifth and Fourteenth Amendments guarantee that no person shall be deprived of life without due process of law."[1]

The real issue at stake in the abortion debate is not freedom of choice, nor the woman's right to privacy, nor even freedom of religion, but the right to life.

In its simplest form, the fundamental question is: Do you believe that a mother has the right to have her pre-born baby killed?

Endnote

1. "PROCLAMATION 5761 OF JANUARY 14, 1988: NATIONAL SANCTITY OF HUMAN LIFE DAY, 1988," Federal Register, Vol. 53, No. 11, Tuesday, January 19, 1988.

Chapter 13

THE FIRST VICTIM

The first and most obvious victim of abortion is the pre-born baby. If the abortion occurs during the first trimester, as most do, the baby is literally vacuumed out of the womb by a powerful suction machine. He is torn apart limb by limb until all that remains is his tiny head. Since it is too large to come through the suction tube itself, the abortionist inserts into the uterus an instrument, called a polyp forceps, which he uses to grasp the free-floating head. When he does, he crushes it. Finally, it too is removed and the abortion is effectively completed.

Quite possibly, you have found my graphic description offensive. It should be, for what we are talking about here is not a medical procedure, but the systematic killing of a defenseless, pre-born child. Even if it could be accomplished painlessly, without trauma, it would be no less offensive.

But it can't be done painlessly, nor without causing trauma, as Paul Fowler points out:

"The methods of abortion are physically violent. Whether it be a sharp, double-edged curette (or knife) by which the child is unceremoniously dissected, or the suction of the inserted tube which tears apart the tiny child, or the burning effect of the injected saline solution on the tender skin of the child while simultaneously poisoning the baby internally — there is no term more appropriate for such cruel methods than violence."[1]

Attorney Mark Belz argues eloquently that abortion is more than violence, more than killing. He presents a strong case for calling it murder, and a particularly heartless form of murder at that. He lists five reasons for coming to this conclusion:

"First, because its victims are innocent by any human standard of justice.

"Second, because its victims are helpless.

"Third, because the order to kill comes from the victim's mother.

"Fourth, because abortion is always a reasoned, intentional, calculated, conspiratorial act . . . . Presumably (or so we are assured by abortion clinics), the decision to abort is not made lightly. The mother and abortionist, supposedly, think it over carefully before they carry it out.

"Fifth, because the abortionist is paid for the killing."[2]

In light of these tragic and undeniable facts, let us work to amend the Constitution in order to protect the pre-born and to do away with abortion once and for all.

Without question, an unplanned pregnancy can be a crisis, but abortion is not the answer. Even as we work to end abortion, we must also work to eliminate crisis pregnancies and to provide support and help for unwed mothers and their children.

Endnotes

1. Paul B. Fowler, *Abortion: Toward an Evangelical Consensus* (Portland, Oregon: Multnomah, 1987), p. 192.

2. Mark Belz, SUFFER THE LITTLE CHILDREN (Westchester, Illinois: Crossway Books, a division of Good News Publishers, 1989), pp. 24, 25.

Chapter 14

THE SECOND VICTIM

As we saw in the last chapter, abortion's first victim, of course, is always the pre-born child. Whether he is killed by suction-aspiration, dilatation and evacuation, salt poisoning (sometimes called saline abortion) or a hysterectomy or caesarean section, there is no way to exaggerate the brutality of his death.

The second victim is the mother. Former abortion clinic operator Carol Everett "...maintains gross malpractice occurs at many clinics, which the medical establishment usually succeeds in covering up."[1] Contrary to the pro-abortion rhetoric about "safe, legal" abortions, she says, "...we were maiming or killing one woman in every 500."[2]

Yet physical injury may be the least serious complication faced by the mother: "In the past few years more and more women have stepped forward to tell, that far from solving their problems, their 'safe, legal' abortions have left them only depressed, guilt-ridden, angry and even suicidal."[3] This malady is referred to as "Post-Abortion Syndrome."[4]

Linda Cochrane eloquently expresses the unrelenting pain of abortion's aftermath when she writes:

"If abortion is so right, why am I feeling guilty and seeking help from psychiatrists and feminist therapists?

"If abortion is so right, why am I needing increased amounts of alcohol and drugs to numb the pain?

"If abortion is so right, why am I so depressed that I think of suicide as a way out?

"If abortion isn't the death of a baby, why was I grieving?"[5]

Another victim of abortion says, "When I was 18 years old...I had an abortion...and the last two years of my life have been a nightmare....Sometimes I just lie in bed all day long, too depressed to get up. I buy baby clothes and toys. In fact, I have a room full of baby accessories. I see children everywhere I go....I don't feel any less guilty today (two years later) than the day I had the abortion. My memories haven't faded...I've tried alcohol, drugs and relationships. Nothing will ever take away my loss or the memories, not even for a little while."[6]

Given these facts, one can only conclude that abortion is an act of violence against both the mother and her child.

Endnotes

1. Don Feder, "Sick of Death," *Pentecostal Evangel* Nov. 27, 1988, p. 13. Used by permission of Heritage Features Syndicate.

2. Ibid.

3. "Post-Abortion Syndrome," an article in the advertising supplement of an Oklahoma City newspaper, produced and paid for by Life Issues, Inc., Jan. 1989, p. 9.

4. Ibid.

5. Ibid.

6. "Memories of My Abortion," an article in the advertising supplement of an Oklahoma City newspaper, produced and paid for by Life Issues, Inc., Jan. 1989, p. 9.

Chapter 15

POST-ABORTION SYNDROME

According to NRLC (National Right to Life Committee) vice-president Wanda Franz, Ph.D., a developmental psychologist: "Therapists have observed irrational fears and depressions linked to abortion experiences and labeled the problem Post-Abortion Syndrome (PAS)."[1]

"Post-Abortion Syndrome is a delayed reaction. Frequently, a woman may not experience any painful emotions until, on the average, five to nine years after the abortion. Many studies purporting to show no lasting adverse post-abortion response (are) simply done too soon.

"Vincent Rue, Ph.D., psychotherapist and researcher, compares Post-Abortion Syndrome to Post Traumatic Distress Disorder, the long-term reaction found in Vietnam veterans who suddenly exhibit pathological behavior years after the war. (Significantly, more than a decade passed after the end of the war before the American Psychological

Association recognized Post Traumatic Distress as an official disorder.)"[2]

Yet, as painful and distressing as Post-Abortion Syndrome may be, it is not the ultimate tragedy for the woman who goes through an abortion. Beyond whatever physical complications she may suffer, beyond her guilt-ridden grief, lies the greatest danger of all — the death of her personal decency.

In order to kill her baby, she must deny her motherhood, she must put to death that part of her nature which bonds her with her child. Or as Clement of Alexandria explained in the second century: women who have an abortion ". . .wholly lose their humanity along with the fetus."[3]

Perhaps Post-Abortion Syndrome signals a ray of hope. If the mother cannot live with what she has done, then there is still a spark of human goodness in her heart. Unfortunately, hard-core feminists and pro-abortion radicals are working hard to eliminate even this shred of decency.

During a television debate on abortion, pro-life advocate Dr. Victor G. Rosenblum was asked if he thought the furor will die down if enough people have abortions and talk openly about them. Rosenblum lowered his head and whispered, " 'Yes, yes, it will, and that will be the saddest day in American history.' "[4]

The desensitizing effect to which he alluded was driven home to me recently while watching a news program on capital punishment. An executioner was asked if it bothered him to "throw the switch."

"Not at all," he replied. "If one of my children did something deserving of the death sentence, it wouldn't bother me to execute them either, and they know it."

Such wanton disregard for human life is the tragic and inevitable consequence of the taking of life. In no way do I mean to equate capital punishment and abortion. I only use this illustration to emphasize the desensitizing effect of the repeated act. When we kill another human being, whether through legal execution or by abortion, something dies inside of us.

Endnotes

1. "Post-Abortion Syndrome," an article in the advertising supplement of an Oklahoma City newspaper, produced and paid for by Life Issues, Inc., Jan. 1989, p. 9.

2. Ibid.

3. *Pedagogues*, ii, 10:95-96, cited in *Abortion: Toward an Evangelical Consensus* (Portland, Oregon: Multnomah Press, 1987), p. 17.

4. John Powell, S.J., *Abortion: The Silent Holocaust* (Valencia, California: Tabor Publishing Company, a division of DLM, Inc., 1981), p. 10.

Chapter 16

WHO WILL WEEP FOR THE BABIES?

Recently I saw a Planned Parenthood advertisement in a national magazine. It was a testimonial which stated, "When I was fifteen, Planned Parenthood saved my life."[1] It was a far too typical story of teenage pregnancy — unplanned, unwanted and out of wedlock. Such pregnancies are regrettable, at best, perhaps even tragic, but surely not grounds for an abortion.

The unfortunate teenager quoted in the ad went on to say: "I don't know what I would have done if abortion wasn't legal. My only choices were a back alley abortion, trying to do it myself, or being a fifteen-year-old mother."[2]

My heart goes out to her, and to the thousands like her. I understand her concern for the impact this will have on her parents. I can identify with her feelings of inadequacy as she considers the responsibilities of parenthood. I think I can even appreciate her concern for her future and her desire to finish her education before getting married and beginning a family. What I can't understand is how she could kill her baby.

We all know that an unborn child has a heart beat by the end of the third week, reacts to stimuli at seven weeks, can grasp an object placed in its palm and suck its thumb at eleven weeks; so how can we ignore the awful pain and suffering it must experience during an abortion?

For example, a physician who performs saline abortions says, " 'All of a sudden one notices that at the time of the saline infusion there is lot of activity in the uterus. That's not fluid currents. That's obviously the fetus being distressed by swallowing the concentrated salt solution and kicking violently — (that's) the death trauma.' "[3]

In an article in *Christianity Today*, Carl Horn, an attorney, writes: "Make no mistake, we are talking about killing — that proceeds in the United States at the rate of 4,000 unborn children a day. And killing that is cold, calculated, and often brutal."[4]

When King Herod killed all the boy children in Bethlehem who were two years old and under (Matt. 2:16), there was weeping and great mourning. His needless slaughter was nothing compared to the scale of death produced by modern America's abortion factories, and yet I can hear hardly a whimper.

Who will weep for the babies? Who, I ask you, will raise their voice in prayer and protest?

Endnotes

1. *Newsweek*, Dec. 16, 1985.

2. Ibid.

3. Carl Horn, "How Freedom of Thought Is Smothered in America," *Christianity Today*, Apr. 6, 1984, p. 16.

4. Ibid.

Chapter 17

ACCESSORIES TO ABORTION

Recently, I received a phone call from a young woman in response to an article I had written. In it I had stated that while I felt great compassion, even sympathy, for those women who found themselves pregnant out of wedlock, I simply could not understand how any woman could kill her own baby. The aforementioned lady who called was more than a little upset and wanted to know why I couldn't understand how a woman might choose abortion under those circumstances.

"Do I hear you saying that you, or someone close to you, once experienced such a predicament personally and chose to have an abortion?"

My gentle question released a flood of pent-up emotion and a stumbling confession. When the young woman's pain had finally spent itself, I said to her:

"It sounds as if you were able to make that decision because your government had betrayed you by passing an immoral law permitting abortion, and then further encouraged you by providing funds to pay for it."

"Yes," she sobbed.

"And," I continued, "you feel that your church also failed you by not speaking out against abortion, by not helping you to realize the awful truth of what you were about to do. Even your 'Christian' parents were no help. Their lack of moral courage only further confused you."

Again she responded with a tearful yes.

I felt close to her then, and a painful compassion moved me to tears.

I have to confess, though, that I still don't understand how any mother can choose to kill her unborn baby. But, after talking with that distraught young lady, I realize, now more than ever, that the responsibility is not hers alone. Her plight and her decision were the product of a series of complex factors which have resulted in a moral vacuum in which there are no absolutes. Consequently, abortion is considered a "private choice" rather than the premeditated killing of an unborn child.

None of this excuses her, or any of the millions like her, but it does indict the government which passed such a law, and the Church which does little or nothing to correct this miscarriage of justice.

In truth, we are all accessories, or perhaps even accomplices, to abortion.

Chapter 18

THE MYTH OF THE COAT HANGER

The recent Supreme Court decision, in the *Webster v. Reproductive Health Services* case, rather than solving anything, has simply made abortion the most explosive social and political issue since the Vietnam War. As with any issue which is so volatile, both sides tend to exaggerate and to resort to inflammatory language.

The "coat hanger" argument is a case in point. Pro-abortion advocates use it to symbolize the self-induced abortion and the carnage that results from it, or the similar problems of illegal "back-alley" abortions. They allude to it repeatedly and milk it for all it is worth.

In truth, the danger it represents is mostly myth. Dr. Nathanson, one of the founders of the National Abortion Rights Action League as mentioned previously, admits as much in his book *Aborting America:*

"...we (the advocates of abortion on demand) generally emphasized the drama of the individual case, not the mass statistics, but when we spoke of the latter it was always '5,000 to 10,000 deaths a year.' "[1]

He then adds: "I confess I knew the figures were totally false....But in the 'morality' of our revolution it was a useful figure, widely accepted...."[2]

Statistics bear him out. In 1972, the last year before the Blackmun era began, the total number of deaths from illegal abortion was only thirty-nine.[3] That's right — thirty-nine!

Of course, not all fatalities resulting from illegal abortions were reported as such, if the attending doctor wanted to protect the family. In light of that Dr. Nathanson estimates the actual number to be about five hundred, with the outside possibility of as many as one thousand.[4]

Now the death of five hundred women, or even a single woman, for that matter, is a most serious concern, to be sure. But it pales dramatically when compared to the 1.5 million unborn who lose their lives every year as a direct result of legalized abortion. Additionally, we must remember that the unborn die through no fault of their own, while the woman seeking an illegal abortion chooses to jeopardize her own life in an attempt to end the life of her pre-born child.

One final thought. Legalizing abortion does not eliminate the risks. In reality, there are probably more deaths and serious complications as a result of legal abortions. Perhaps not a higher percentage, but certainly a greater total number.

In *Grand Illusions*, his well-documented expose' on Planned Parenthood, George Grant writes:

"Planned Parenthood claims that its efforts to provide abortion services have at last removed the specter of dangerous back alley abortions from our land. But that is an illusion.

"The specter remains, darker and more ominous than ever before.

"The truth is, many of the butchers who ran the old back alley operations have simply moved uptown to ply their grisly trade for Planned Parenthood.

"The same unsafe techniques, the same lecherous motivations, and the same twisted and perverse ethics that marred their criminal careers continue to haunt them."[5]

Dr. Horton Dean, a gynecologist with a private practice in a fashionable neighborhood near Los Angeles concurs with Mr. Grant. He says, "I am convinced that the Planned Parenthood programs pose the greatest health hazard in America today."[6] He estimates that as many as fifteen percent of all first trimester, forty percent of all mid-trimester, and ninety percent of all late-trimester abortions result in problems demanding serious medical attention.[7]

So much for the myth of the coat hanger.

Endnotes

1. Bernard N. Nathanson, M.D., with Richard N. Ostling, *Aborting America* (Garden City, New York: Doubleday and Company, 1979), p. 193.

2. Ibid.

3. Ibid.

4. Ibid.

5. George Grant, *Grand Illusions* (Brentwood, Tennessee: Wolgemuth & Hyatt, 1988), p. 33.

6. Ibid., pp. 65, 66.

7. Ibid.

Chapter 19

PRO-CHOICE BY DEFAULT

Tragically only a tormented few see abortion for what it is: the murder of an unborn child! This terrible truth is often obscured by a host of irrelevant questions and euphemistic rhetoric. The fact that the actual execution is accomplished in a modern clinic, or hospital, under the guise of medical treatment only further complicates the public's ability to perceive it for what it is. The plight of the unborn is further obscured by the fact that the tiny victims are invisible to everyone but the abortionist. Their silent screams are never heard.

While this does not excuse us, it may explain our reticence to become involved. Let me illustrate:

Recently I interviewed the Reverend Paul Schenck, President of the National Clergy Council for Operation Rescue. In the course of our conversation, I asked him how he became involved in the rescue movement. His answer haunts me still:

"I suppose I've always been pro-life by conviction," he replied, "but in truth I was pro-choice by default. I paid lip service to those who opposed abortion, but I never really did anything about it. That is, until about two years ago.

"It all started when a young couple came to my office to see me. They placed a garbage bag on my desk and told me to open it. Inside were the mutilated bodies of four aborted babies. They were disemboweled. Their tiny arms and legs had been torn from their torsos. They had been decapitated.

"For the very first time I realized what abortion really was — the deliberate, premeditated murder of a pre-born baby. For years I had heard the numbers: fifteen million, eighteen million, twenty-two million, but they were just that — numbers. Now I knew better. On my desk was the gruesome evidence! I couldn't pretend any longer."

Following that experience, Paul became active in the rescue movement. His commitment has not been without its consequences. At last count he had been arrested some thirteen times for nonviolently attempting to save the unborn from certain death at the hands of the abortionist. He took part in the Atlanta rescue during the 1988 Democratic National Convention and ended up being arrested and jailed. Most recently he was sentenced to twenty days in jail for a rescue in which he and other pastors chained themselves together inside an abortion clinic. They succeeded in closing it down for an entire day thus saving the lives of several babies who were scheduled to be killed.

Unfortunately, there are far too few who see abortion for what it really is and respond accordingly. Even those of us who are pro-life by conviction are far too often pro-choice by default. While we may be personally opposed to abortion, we aren't willing to do anything about it.

What, I wonder, will it take for the rest of us to wake up and realize that our nation is systematically murdering our pre-born children? What will it take to arouse us to intervene on their behalf? As macabre as it may sound, I almost wish everyone of us could be forced to witness the results of an abortion first hand. Perhaps then we could come to grips with the awful horrors of what America is doing to her unborn. You can be sure that history will one day ask us, as it now does of the Germans: "Why didn't you do something to stop the killing?"

Dr. James Dobson, of "Focus on the Family," put both abortion and our Christian responsibility in historic perspective when he said, "After World War II, German citizens living around Nazi extermination camps were required to visit the facilities to witness the atrocities they had permitted to occur. Though it was technically 'legal' to kill Jews and other political prisoners, the citizens were blamed for not breaking the law in deference to a higher moral code.

"This is the way we feel about the slaughter of twenty-five million unborn children. Some of them are being burned to death by a salt solution only days before a normal delivery would have occurred. This is a moral outrage that transcends the law which sanitizes the killings.

"We are law-abiding people and do not advocate violence or obscene and disrespectful behavior, but, to be sure, we will follow that higher moral code nonviolently, to rescue innocent, defenseless babies.

"And some day, the moral issues involved here will be as clear to the world as the Nazi holocaust is today."[1]

Endnote

1. From "Focus on the Family" broadcast, Aug. 12, 1988.

Chapter 20

ANSWERING THE CALL

Some time ago I was speaking to a right-to-life rally. When I had finished, a young woman came to the front of the auditorium and asked to speak to the audience. Noting her obvious distress, I hesitated before giving her the microphone.

Tearfully she confessed that eight years earlier she had aborted her baby. It was a now all too familiar story of a child conceived out of wedlock. The father had wanted nothing more to do with the young woman or her unborn child. In shame and desperation she had scheduled a legal and inexpensive abortion.

This is where her story took an unusual turn.

Trembling, she told us that on the way to the abortion clinic she had "prayed" that someone would stop her.

"If only one person had asked me not to do it," she sobbed, "my baby would be alive today.

"I can't go back and undo what I've done," she continued. "but I pledge to you, and to God, that I will be there, in front of the abortion clinic, to help some other woman save her baby."

Listening to her story, I couldn't help but wonder how many other babies have been killed simply because no one was there.

In his introduction to Randall Terry's book, *Operation Rescue,* Dr. D. James Kennedy writes: "The shocking reality is that Christians could stop abortions today, if they wanted to.

"If four million Christians went tomorrow and stood as a visible presence in front of every abortion clinic in the land, no babies would be killed. Even if everyone were arrested for this courageous stand for God's truth, our already overcrowded jails would not be able to hold this number."

He then exhorts us not to ". . . repeat the lesson of the German church in the 1930s and '40s that stood apathetically by and watched as the unwanted of their generation were marched off to unspeakable death. We need Corrie ten Booms of the 1980s who will stand up to man's repudiation of God's law and follow Jesus' command to love our neighbors as ourselves."[1]

Endnote

1. Dr. D. James Kennedy, Foreword to *Operation Rescue* by Randall A. Terry (Springdale, Pennsylvania: Whitaker House, 1988).

Chapter 21

UNLIKELY HEROES: JOAN ANDREWS

To the abortion clinic operator, she is the enemy — a right-to-life radical. To the law enforcement officers and the judicial system, she is an embarrassing nuisance. To the general public, she is an enigma — a sensitive and caring person, a devout Christian, a model citizen in virtually every way. And yet since 1973 she has been arrested scores of times, in several states, for her non-violent attempts to stop abortion.

To the unborn, that makes her a hero!

In 1986 a Florida judge sentenced her to five years in prison. (It is interesting to note that later that same day this judge handed down four-year sentences to two men convicted of being accessories to murder.)

In an order explaining his reason for giving her the severest penalty allowed by law, Judge William Anderson wrote:

"This defendant has a long record of trespass and invasion of the property of others, which is of escalating seriousness. The record and the defendant's own statements disclose that for several years her only business has been going from state to state for the purpose of committing such criminal acts. The defendant has consistently advised the Court that she would not obey the conditions of any probation, but unless confined she will continue to commit further criminal acts, as she is not bound by the laws that bind others. For these reasons, no probation, community control, or lenient sentence will serve to end her criminal conduct, and a lengthy period of incarceration is necessary."[1]

Is Joan Andrews a common criminal, or a true hero of the faith?

To answer that question, you and I will have to come to grips with the ugly reality of abortion and the pressing issue of our individual moral responsibility. If we believe that all life is a gift from God, and therefore sacred, then we cannot ignore the killing of the pre-born which goes on in America's abortion clinics at the rate of four to five thousand a day.

In truth, the enormity of what abortion represents demands something more than pickets and political protest, magazine articles and sermons. Not less than, but more than. For Joan Andrews that "something more" means placing her body between the killing machinery of the abortion clinic and the defenseless pre-born baby!

Endnote

1. *State of Florida v. Joan Elizabeth Andrews,* in the Circuit Court in and for Escambia County, Florida, Case No. 86-1663-CFAS, Order of William H. Anderson, Circuit Judge, Sept. 25, 1986.

Chapter 22

UNLIKELY HEROES: CHRISTY ANNE COLLINS

Christy Anne Collins has been arrested nearly fifty times and has spent many months in jail. Yet she is not your common criminal. Quite to the contrary, she is a member of a large evangelical Episcopal church and heads the Sanctity of Life Ministries in Annandale, Virginia. The thing that gets Christy in trouble is her commitment to protect the rights of the pre-born.

Like Joan Andrews, she does not believe abortion is simply an issue. An issue is something that can be resolved by negotiation and compromise. Nor is abortion a "mere" legal matter to be decided by the Supreme Court. Rather it is a matter of life and death. And thus it demands the ultimate commitment on the part of those conscientious persons who would see it stopped.

Christy explained her position to Judge Richard Salzman of the District of Columbia Superior Court when she appeared before him for sentencing on May 16, 1988:

"Your Honor, you have, throughout the trial, talked about the laws of this land. The fundamental right of every American citizen is the right to life; a right our Constitution declares an unalienable right endowed by our Creator. It is not something you or I or the state can choose to give or take away.

"Whether a person is pre-born, dying of AIDS, mentally incompetent, retarded, physically handicapped or otherwise not perfect, or unwanted by some, life is not something we can choose to throw away or minimize.

". . .Your Honor, I want you to know I respect the law greatly. I respect the law that says every human being, every American citizen, has the unalienable right to life. I am not called to yield my conscience to the legislature and I am not called to elevate the state to the place of God in my life.

"If the laws of this courtroom and the laws of the land that sanction the brutal murder of an unborn child become more important than the fact that these children are made in the image of God, and are children He would protect, then I will have failed at what is most important in my life: obedience to God.

". . .I am not an evil person. I am not a criminal. And I do not belong in your jail, except under your standard of justice which protects murder and convicts those who act in defense of life."[1]

Whereupon she was fined $150 and sentenced to nine months in jail.

I, for one, am proud of Christy Anne Collins and of the hundreds like her who are willing to suffer both reproach and imprisonment in an effort to end abortion. She makes me think of the Apostle Peter who wrote: "If you suffer, it should not be as a murderer or thief or any other kind of criminal, or even as a meddler. However, if you suffer as a Christian, do not be ashamed, but praise God that you bear that name" (1 Pet. 4:15,16).

Endnote

1. Mark Belz, *SUFFER THE LITTLE CHILDREN* (Westchester, Illinois: Crossway Books, a Division of Good News Publishers, 1989), pp. 39,40.

Chapter 23

UNLIKELY HEROES:
JOE WALL

Joe Wall is a rather ordinary-looking sixty-year-old man with a failing heart. He is a senior auditor by profession — that is, he was until he was fired from the Philadelphia city controller's office for being "AWOL."

He was absent because he was in jail for trespassing on the property of an abortion clinic in an attempt to save the pre-born from certain death. Although he had forty-eight vacation days coming, his request for vacation time to cover his absence was purposely denied by his superior who terminated him after he had missed five consecutive days of work.

Given an opportunity to address the court just prior to his sentencing, he said:

"Now that the legal process has ended, we can dispense with the pretense, with the sham, that this prosecution had nothing to do with the subject of abortion. This was the substantive issue; everyone in this courtroom knows it. It is time we addressed it. The only reason we went into that clinic that day was to attempt to stop the killing, the murder, of innocent unborn children. It beggars common sense to say that fifteen people would walk into a clinic and stay there for no reason at all...I know I would not have been there, ...for any other reason, given my age, fifty-nine, my bad heart, my professional background.

"I, and the other fourteen of us, went into that abortion clinic to take one small step to help fight an evil so immense that it is hard to grasp, difficult to comprehend. And that is a large part of the problem. Most people can't comprehend it; they don't even want to think about it.

"Just for the moment think about it. Twenty million or more human beings killed since 1973. Torn to pieces, shredded into garbage, burned to death. That's the reality we have to live with, to try to face.

"...In the face of an incredible tragedy like this, any charges of trespass shrink into insignificance. To say that, in attempting to halt this blood bath, we must blindly and mindlessly follow the letter of the law, without regard to whether it is just or not, among other things makes a mockery of our whole American history....

"The point of this is that the idea that you can separate a particular action in technical violation of the law from the reason for it makes no sense whatever. For one who thinks that way, a major portion of American history is no more than a criminal conspiracy."[1]

Joe Wall's case is being appealed, but that's hardly the point. It's his life, his commitment, which appeals to all of us who claim to believe that abortion is the killing of pre-born children. If we really believe that to be true, then isn't it time we made the kind of life-sacrifice such a belief demands?

In the days ahead, a prison record for criminal trespass at an abortion clinic will become a spiritual virtue rather than a cause for shame. As Jaime Cardinal Sin, Archbishop of Manila, so aptly put it: "How often an imprisonment has radically changed the direction of national or global affairs. Take away the names of all the noble prisoners from history, and there will not be enough spiritual energy to run the world."[2]

Endnotes

1. Mark Belz, *SUFFER THE LITTLE CHILDREN* (Westchester, Illinois: Crossway Books, a Division of Good News Publishers, 1989), pp. 51-53.

2. Jaime Cardinal Sin, Archbishop of Manila, quoted in *THE PRISON LETTERS OF JOAN ANDREWS*, Joan Andrews, edited by Richard Cowden-Guido (Brentwood, Tennessee: Wolgemuth & Hyatt, Publishers, Inc., 1988).

Chapter 24

WHAT DOES GOD EXPECT OF ME?

Not long ago I had an opportunity to interview Joseph Forman, the Southeast Regional Director for Operation Rescue. During the course of that discussion, I asked him how he became involved in rescue. He told me that he had been active in the pro-life movement for more than ten years when he realized that he needed to do something more than picket.

It was Saturday morning, and he was preparing to leave for the abortion clinic where he planned to spend the day picketing and doing sidewalk counseling along with other pro-lifers. Noticing that he was about to leave, his seven-year-old daughter tearfully asked, "Daddy, why do you have to go again?"

Kneeling down, he took her little-girl hands in his and said, gently, "Sweetheart, they're killing babies in there, and someone has to try to make them stop."

With a seven-year-old's innocence she responded, "Daddy, if they're really killing babies, why don't you do something more than just carry that silly old sign?"

Listening to him recount that pivotal encounter, I think I felt something of the conviction that must have gripped him. I say I believe that abortion is the killing of pre-born children, but do I really believe that? If I did — if I do — then what does God expect of me?

If I were aware that my neighbor was planning to kill his four-week-old child, and if I knew the exact time and place it was to happen, what would be my reasonable responsibility? I could try to talk him out of his grisly plan, but if that failed I would need to take more drastic action. Not only would I be justified in intervening to save the life of his child, I would be found negligent if I didn't.

Now let's complicate that situation just a little. Suppose the law gave him the right to kill his infant child if he so chose. Would the fact that the murder of infants is now legal absolve me of my God-given responsibility?

Hardly!

What we are talking about here is not civil disobedience, but divine obedience. I must love that infant as myself, and I must lay down my life for him, even if that means disobeying an immoral law!

Or as attorney Mark Belz so eloquently argues in regard to the believer's response to abortion:

"Does not moral integrity demand, in addition to the essential works of evangelism, adoption, opening homes to unwed mothers, and so forth, that some kind of immediate protection be given those individuals, that some action be taken — something beyond words?"[1]

Endnote

1. Mark Belz, *SUFFER THE LITTLE CHILDREN* (Westchester, Illinois: Crossway Books, a Division of Good News Publishers, 1989), p. 31.

protection be given these individuals, that some action be taken — something beyond words."

Endnote

1. Mark Bubeck, THE ADVERSARY (Westchester, Illinois Crossway Books, a Division of Good News Publishers, 1989), p. 81.

Chapter 25

SELF-INTEREST

As I have become increasingly aware of the enormity of the abortion holocaust, I have found myself asking how such a thing could happen in America.

My question usually takes two forms. The first focuses on the mother and asks, "How can she kill her own baby?" The second focuses on those of us who claim to be pro-life; it asks, "Why don't we rise up en masse and put an end to the killing?"

The answers, I've discovered, are frighteningly similar.

An overwhelming number of abortions are performed for the sake of personal convenience. The principals involved (i.e. the mother, her parents, even the baby's father) see abortion as a simple solution to an embarrassing and inconvenient situation. The mother, often with the encouragement of her parents and the baby's father, chooses her education, her career, her freedom, even her reputation, over the life of her unborn baby. In short, she sacrifices her pre-born baby's life to her own self-interests.

In light of that truth, we can only conclude that, at its roots, abortion is raw selfishness!

Now we must ask ourselves why we are not more involved in putting an end to the abortion holocaust. The answer, I'm afraid, is simply a matter of self-interest.

Fighting abortion is a thankless task with high risks. If we become involved in it, we will be misunderstood, not infrequently, by our Christian friends, and even our own family. If we choose to participate in rescue activities, we will probably be arrested and, if we persist, even jailed. We risk both our career and our family's financial security.

If these issues are considered abstractly, they make a good case for not becoming personally involved. But when we weigh them against the life of a single baby, they can only be described as self-serving.

When we continue to place our own self-interests ahead of the welfare of the pre-born child, does this not say something about the kind of people we are?

In her decision to abort, the mother demonstrates that she places more value on her self-interests than on the life of her baby. When we do not intervene on behalf of the pre-born, it is generally for the same reason. At the root of the mother's choice to abort, and our choice not to intervene, lies the same thing — self-interest.

Chapter 26

THE BEAST WITHIN

Once the veil of the pro-choice propaganda is pierced and the atrocities of abortion, in all of their bloody horror, are exposed, it is easy to become enraged. But we must never allow our "righteous indignation" unguided expression. To do so is to become a monster in our effort to destroy the monster of abortion.

In an article in *Christianity Today*, Philip Yancey relates an incident which I believe illustrates this truth.

According to Yancey, a pastor friend of his served in the Army during the closing days of World War II and participated in the liberation of the infamous Dachau concentration camp.

He later told Yancy that the most shocking part of the whole experience was not the atrocities which the SS officers had perpetrated upon the helpless Jews, though such cruelty was beyond human imagination. The thing that stayed with him was what he discovered about himself.

The captain of the liberating forces asked for someone to escort twelve SS prisoners to the interrogation center. The most volatile soldier in the unit, a man named Chuck, eagerly volunteered. Grabbing a submachine gun, he herded the captives down the trail where they soon disappeared into some trees in a shallow ravine. Shortly thereafter, a burst of machine gun fire shattered the afternoon stillness. In a few minutes, Chuck swaggered back and announced with a kind of fiendish leer, "They all tried to escape."

In that moment, Yancey's friend experienced a nauseating fear that he might be called upon to escort the next group of SS guards to the interrogation center. The thing he feared most was that he too might give in to his unspeakable rage and gun down the guards as Chuck had done.

"The beast that was within those guards," he said, "was also within me."

In our efforts to stop abortion, we must never give into the beast that is within each of us. One act of violence, one fit of temper, one moment of hate, and the monster is loose.

Personally, I have found it very helpful to remind myself that the abortion clinic operator is not my enemy, nor is the abortionist, nor the mother seeking an abortion. Jesus loves them just as much as He loves me.

Remember, we are called to overcome evil with good. (Rom. 12:21.)

Chapter 27

THE CRY OF THE UNBORN

During the past sixteen years, more than twenty-five million pre-born babies have been killed by abortion in the United States alone. If you will allow me to be so presumptuous, I would like to speak on their behalf. Not simply for them, but as one of them — at least, as their representative, as their "voice from the grave."

To the abortionists, I say: "Remember your Hippocratic oath. You have sworn an oath to be a healer, a protector of life.

"In our scientific age, your word, your judgment, is like a moral law. If you say that killing by abortion is not really killing, if you say that it is merely the expelling of the product of conception, then it is so in the hearts and minds of your patients.

"But regardless of whether you call it killing or not, my life has been terminated. Whatever method of abortion you choose, we, the helpless victims, experience the trauma of death in all of its unspeakable pain and horror.

"I challenge you to stand against the tide of public opinion and affirm the sanctity of life. Use your medical knowledge and the scientific evidence at your disposal to show that life begins at conception. If you will do so, maybe this terrible holocaust can be stopped.

"Above all, I urge you not to allow rationalization or greed to make you deaf to our cries. Have mercy upon us, I pray. Have mercy."

To the legislators, I say: "Be persons of courage and integrity. Enact laws which reflect that which is most noble in humankind; laws which challenge your constituents to be their best selves; laws which stay the fallen nature — the selfish, inhuman nature — which is a tragic fact of humanity. Left to their own desires, people will selfishly kill and destroy.

"Do not simply rely upon your own wisdom, for you too are mere humans afflicted with the same shortcomings as other men and women. Draw upon the wisdom of God and enact laws embodying the eternal principles of the Judeo-Christian ethic.

"I urge you to remember that you are not simply enacting statutes, but shaping the soul of our nation."

To the pregnant woman considering an abortion, I say: "Consider what you are about to do. Although I am a distinct and separate human being in my own right, I am also flesh of your flesh, bone of your bone, and life of your life. Kill me, and you kill something of yourself. When I die, something inside of you dies. Life will never be the same. To have an abortion, you must violate the maternal instinct which is an inherent part of your personhood; to do away with me, you must deny a part of who you are.

"Yes, your situation is inconvenient at best, perhaps even desperate, but it hardly justifies the taking of my life. Perhaps those you love and trust have counseled you to have an abortion. Maybe they have said that is a simple solution to a complicated situation. Well, it may be the 'easiest answer,' but it is not the best answer, and it is a decision you will regret all the days of your life."

To the Church, I say: "How long will you ignore the sin of abortion? How long will you close your eyes to the atrocities which are being perpetrated upon the unborn? How long will you protect your status quo at our expense?

"Lift up your voice in both prayer and protection. Not shrilly in anger, but passionately in Christian concern. Concern for the aborted and the abortionist alike, for both mother and child — in love for all of God's creation.

"Open your hearts and your homes to these unwed mothers. Give them a loving alternative. Risk being misunderstood. Risk being persecuted and imprisoned.

"Risk everything, for greater love has no one than this, that one lay down his life for others." (John 15:13.)

"I do not speak for myself alone, but for all of the unborn — both those who have already been murdered by abortion, and those who face that risk in the future. For the twenty-five million who have already died, and for the millions more who will be conceived only to face this same violent and untimely end."

Chapter 28

The final victim

As we have seen, the two most obvious victims of abortion are the defenseless pre-born child and the mother herself.

The pre-born child is violently dragged from his mother's womb to a brutal death. The mother often suffers both physical and psychological complications. She is locked in a prison of pain, and all the court decisions and popular euphemisms, which made her decision to have an abortion so easy, cannot help her now. All she can remember is how it felt when the doctor inserted the long needle directly into her womb in order to inject the saline solution, and then the frantic convulsions of her baby as he died. Later her own pains came as she struggled to deliver her dead child.

Then there's the constant battle with nightmares. Sometimes they go on for years. Dreams in which babies are seen floating down drains, or being pickled in jars, or experimented upon. Dreams of a second chance, of what might have been.

91

To make matters worse, there is the sense of guilt which is experienced every time the subject of abortion comes up.

Plus the feeling of anger and remorse, the tormented questions: "Why didn't someone stop me? Why didn't someone help me? Why didn't someone tell me it would be like this?"

And finally there is the overwhelming sense of loss, the never-ending thoughts: "She would be almost seven now. . . . he would be entering kindergarten this year. . . ."

The final victim is not so obvious and her ultimate demise may not be complete for some time yet. I'm talking about the moral conscience of our nation, the soul of the American people, that sense of decency and reverence for life which defines the texture and quality of life as we know it.

Even now we are witnessing the death throes. Beneath the obvious hedonism there is an even more fundamental disregard for the sanctity of life. Violence abounds. The abuse and exploitation of children is proliferating. There are no moral absolutes, no objective standards upon which society can found her governing values. As a consequence, America is fast becoming a nation without a soul.

Abortion on demand is both a consequence and a cause.

It is a consequence in that it could never have been legalized if those in power had not already adopted a dehumanizing philosophy of life — a new "ethic" which holds that there is such a thing as a life not worthy to be allowed to live.

Historically, we find this same "fatal first step" at the heart of the Nazi holocaust. It began, not with the Jews, but with ". . .the aged, the infirm, the senile and mentally retarded, and defective children. Eventually, as World War II approached, the doomed undesirables included epileptics, World War I amputees, children with badly modeled ears, and even bed wetters."[1]

Abortion is a cause in that, in order to allow the killing of defenseless pre-born babies, legal action had to be taken which resulted in the devaluation of the whole of life.

As John Powell, S.J., observed in regard to the *Roe v. Wade* decision: "The terrible indifference toward human life in that decision, and especially the language of Justice Blackmun about a 'meaningful life,' would seem to make all the other forms of killing simple logical corollaries."[2]

In other words, if children are only the "products of conception," then the traditional values which gave them dignity and which protected them as human beings have been irrevocably amended.

"In 1975, The Sonoma (California) Conference on Ethical Issues in Neonatal Intensive Care published a 193-page report entitled 'Ethics of Newborn Intensive Care.' During the conference, it was reported, a panel of twenty people in the health care field was asked: 'Would it be right to directly intervene to kill a (severely defective though) self-sustaining infant?' (Note: A self-sustaining infant is one who can live without technical assistance of any kind. This baby can survive with no help other than normal feeding.) Seventeen of the twenty panelists agreed that such direct intervention would be a permissible option. They answered yes to the question. It is sadly interesting to note that the three physicians on the panel said that they would hesitate to kill such a self-sustaining infant directly, but would not prevent someone else from doing the killing.

"Dr. R.T.F. Schmidt, at that time president-elect of the American College of Obstetrics and Gynecologists, when asked about the consensus of the Sonoma Conference, had this to say: 'The fact that seventeen of the twenty expert panelists believe that some severely defective infants should be killed under certain conditions is not only deeply disturbing to our traditional concept of the inherent value of human life but is potentially shattering to the foundations of Western civilization.' "[3]

One can only predict a bleak future for these people and for ourselves.

In ways more frightening than we might imagine, the future is now: ". . . state courts in 1987 ruled for the first time that patients could be starved to death, even without their permission, if their family decides that's probably what the patient would want — and this, even if the family stands economically to benefit. Infanticide, though theoretically restrained by law(s) . . . in fact made eerie advances: For the first time, hospitals agreed to keep children scheduled for abortion alive until after a forced premature birth so that their body parts could be cut out (while they are still alive) in order to assist the health of others."[4]

Perhaps Dr. Leon R. Kass, professor of the Liberal Arts of Human Biology at the University of Chicago, put it best when he said: ". . . we are already witnessing the erosion of our idea of man as something splendid or divine, as a creature with freedom and dignity. And clearly, if we come to see ourselves as meat, then meat we shall become."[5]

In the end, those who support abortion, infanticide, and euthanasia, *as well as those who simply allow these things to be performed*, will make life itself the final victim.

Endnotes

1. Francis A. Schaeffer and C. Everett Koop, M.D., *Whatever Happened to the Human Race?* (Old Tappan, New Jersey: Fleming H. Revell Company, 1979), p. 106.

2. John Powell, S.J., *Abortion: The Silent Holocaust* (Valencia, California: Tabor Publishing Company, a division of DLM, Inc., 1981), p. 39. Taken from article by Dr. R.T.F. Schmidt, *Pediatric News,* April 1977.

3. Ibid., pp. 47, 48.

4. Joan Andrews, Richard Cowden-Guido, Ed., *THE PRISON LETTERS OF JOAN ANDREWS* (Brentwood, Tennessee: Wolgemuth & Hyatt, Publishers, Inc., 1988), p. 2.

5. Dr. Leon R. Kass, "Making Babies — The New Biology and the 'Old' Morality," *The Public Interest*, Winter 1972, p. 53.

Chapter 29

A CHRISTIAN RESPONSE

A few weeks ago I was having breakfast with some members of the official board from Christian Chapel where I serve as senior pastor. During the course of the conversation, one of the board members said to me, "It's readily apparent that you intend to become very involved in the fight to outlaw abortion."

I nodded a response, so he continued. "What do you expect from us?"

I thought for a moment, then replied: "I expect you to do exactly as the Holy Spirit asks you to do! Additionally, I expect you to guard our unity. The enemy would like to divide the Body by generating a controversy over the 'scriptural' way to stop abortion. If he can get us to expend our energies in these peripheral issues, then we will be unable to concentrate on the task at hand.

"If, in good conscience, you feel that you cannot risk civil disobedience to save the lives of the pre-born, then I accept that decision. There are many legal ways of fighting abortion. By the same token, I ask you to respect those who choose to risk all in a non-violent effort to stop the killing."

Remember, "If a house is divided against itself, that house cannot stand" (Mark 3:25).

Prayer is the first and most obvious way of becoming involved. But having said that, let me hasten to add that prayer must not be the Church's only involvement. To pray and do nothing else would be a serious mistake, not unlike trying to evangelize the world through prayer alone. No sincere Christian would be so naive. To win the lost we must add witness and service to our intercession. To end abortion we must add involvement and intervention to our prayers.

The abortion conflict, as any sincere Christian knows, is more than a political issue, more than a social issue. It is a spiritual battle:

"For our struggle is not against flesh and blood, but against the rulers, against the authorities, against the power of this dark world and against the spiritual forces of evil in the heavenly realms" (Eph. 6:12).

Still, we must not lose sight of the fact that this battle is also being waged in both the social and political arenas. It will not be won unless we first win the spiritual battle in prayer. But, by the same token, we must leave the prayer closet to do battle in both the political realm and at the door of the abortion clinic itself!

In addition to prayer and witnessing, there is political action, legal picketing, and sidewalk counseling. Some of us may want to become involved as volunteer counselors, or serve as support personnel for a local Life Alternative program. Others may choose to become a host family for a woman who is in the midst of a crisis pregnancy.

As Pope John Paul II told a group of pilgrims in Rome on January 3, 1979: "The pregnant woman must not be left alone with her doubts, her difficulties, her temptations. We must stand with her, so that she might have the necessary courage and faith. . . ."

And some of us may even want to adopt an "unwanted" baby.

Finally, there is rescue.

Please do not confuse Operation Rescue with a demonstration or a protest. It is neither. It is exactly what its name implies — a rescue effort!

In this activity, conscientious persons place their bodies between the mother seeking an abortion and the clinic itself. Support personnel are also available to counsel with any woman who is prevented from ending the life of her pre-born infant. Not infrequently, she is convinced to carry her baby to term, and thus a "rescue" is accomplished — a pre-born baby is saved from certain death!

A secondary benefit is the "prophetic" witness the rescuer's presence produces. No longer can the abortionist, or the mother seeking an abortion, commit these dark deeds under the cloak of anonymity. By virtue of their presence, rescuers shine the light of God's truth on the holocaust against the unborn. As a result, the entire community is called to account. No longer can the members of that community pretend ignorance of this great evil.

Those who attempt such rescue operations are often accused of civil disobedience. But that is not really the case, at least not in the strictest sense of the word. Civil disobedience is a deliberate violation of an unjust law, committed as a means of drawing attention to that law, in order to provoke the enactment of a legal change. Rescue, on the other hand, focuses on spiritual obedience. The law, or laws, which the rescuers break are incidental to their task. They are simply obeying God in an attempt to rescue the pre-born from certain death.

The purity of their intent, however, in no way protects rescuers from the consequences of their actions. Not only are they hated by the personnel of the abortion clinic, they are often misunderstood by fellow believers as well. When arrested they are fined and often jailed. With increasing frequency the judicial system is meting out the stiffest penalties allowed by law.

The battle lines have been clearly drawn, and it is now time for all of us who name the name of Jesus to take our places in rank. We are facing a moral challenge not unlike that which confronted the founding fathers of our country more than two hundred years ago. In their moment of truth, they found the strength to risk their very lives. Each man who signed the Declaration of Independence knew that he was signing his death warrant. If the revolution failed, he would be hunted down and hanged as a traitor to the Crown.

Yet the alternative was unthinkable — a life without freedom!

Perhaps Patrick Henry expressed it best in his address at St. John's Church on March 23, 1775:

" 'Shall we try argument? . . . Shall we resort to entreaty? . . . What terms shall we find which have not been already exhausted?...We have petitioned, we have remonstrated, we have supplicated....We have been spurned with contempt....There is no longer any room for hope....Is life so dear or peace so sweet as to be purchased at the price of chains?...Forbid it, Almighty God!...I know not what course others may take, but as for me, give me liberty or give me death!' "[1]

In a like vein, I ask you: Is your life so dear, is the status quo so sweet, is your career so precious, as to be purchased at the price of twenty-five million unborn babies? Is the favor of unregenerate men and women so important that we will choose it at the price of one and a half million unborn babies every year? God forbid!

May we speak as with one voice: "I know not what course others may take, but as for me, I am going to speak up for those who cannot speak for themselves. With all that is within me, I am going to defend the cause of the weak and the fatherless. I am going to speak prophetically to maintain the rights of the poor and the oppressed. I am going to do everything within my power, non-violently, to rescue the pre-born, to deliver them from certain death at the hand of the abortionist. This I will do, whatever the cost, so help me God!"

Endnote

1. Paul Aurandt, *Paul Harvey's The Rest of the Story* (New York: A Bantam Book, published by arrangement with Doubleday and Company, 1977), pp. 21, 22.

PRAYER

Oh, God, forgive us, for we have sinned.

Some of us have committed the sin of abortion. Cleanse us from blood guiltiness.

Some of us have committed the sin of negligence. We have not lifted our voices either in protest or in prayer on behalf of the unborn. Their blood is on our hands. Forgive us and cleanse us.

Some of us have committed the sin of hatred. We have hated the abortionists, those who advocate abortion, and those who have had an abortion. Forgive us, O Lord, and give us Your holy love.

Heal our land, and return us to righteousness.

In the name of Jesus, I pray.

Amen.

PRO-LIFE ORGANIZATIONS

The list below is based largely on the list of pro-life organizations in the book, *Grand Illusions*, by George Grant.[1] "Each has literature, presentations, services, resources, and opportunities" of which you can take advantage. Also "each is deserving of your prayerful and financial support."

Advocates for Life*
P. O. Box 13656
Portland, OR 97213

Americans Against Abortion*
P. O. Box 40
Lindale, TX 75771

American Life League (ALL)*
P. O. Box 490
Stafford, VA 22554

Americans United for Life*
343 S. Dearborn, Suite 1804
Chicago, IL 60604

Biblical Action League
P. O. Box 574
Catoosa, OK 74015

Birthright*
11235 S. Western Ave.
Chicago, IL 60643

Black Americans for Life*
419 7th St. N.W., Suite 402
Washington, DC 20004

Christian Action Council (CAC)*
422 C St. N.E.
Washington, DC 20002

Clergy Council — Tulsa
7807 E. 76th St.
Tulsa, OK 74133

Committee to Protect
the Family Foundation*
8001 Forbes Place, Suite 102
Springfield, VA 22151

Concerned Women for America
(CWA)*
122 C St. N.W., Suite 800
Washington, DC 20001

Couple to Couple League*
P. O. Box 11084
Cincinnati, OH 45211

---

*From *Grand Illusions*.

Eagle Forum*
P. O. Box 618
Alton, IL 62002

Family Research Council*
515 Second St. N.E.
Washington, DC 20002

Focus on the Family*
801 Corporate Center Drive
Pomona, CA 91764

Free Congress Research and
Education Foundation*
721 Second St. N.E.
Washington, DC 20002

Heart Light*
P. O. Box 8513
Green Bay, WI 54308

HELP Services Women's Center*
P. O. Box 1141
Humble, TX 77338

Human Life Foundation*
150 East 35th Street
New York, NY 10157

Human Life International*
7845-E Airpark Road
Gaithersburg, MD 20879

Liberty Federation*
505 Second Street, N.E.
Washington, DC 20002

Liberty Godparent Foundation*
P. O. Box 27000
Lynchburg, VA 24506

Life Advocates*
4848 Guiton, Suite 209
Houston, TX 77027

Life Alternative
2651 E. 21st St., Suite 407
Tulsa, OK 74114

LifeNet*
P. O. Box 185066
Fort Worth, TX 76181-0066

March for Life Education
  and Defense Fund*
P.O. Box 90330
Washington, DC 20090

March Houston for Life*
P. O. Box 207
Spring, TX 77383

Moral Majority*
2020 Tate Springs Road
Lynchburg, VA 24501

National Right to Life Committee*
419 7th St. N.W., Suite 402
Washington, DC 20004

Operation Blessing*
CBN Center
Virginia Beach, VA 23463

Operation Rescue
P. O. Box 1180
Binghamton, NY 13902

Orthodox Christians for Life*
P. O. Box 805
Melville, NY 11747

Pearson Institute
3663 Lindell Blvd., Suite 290
St. Louis, MO 63108

Project Rescue — Tulsa
Mark Crow
1801 W. Willow
Broken Arrow, OK 74012

Pro-Life Action League*
6160 N. Cicero Ave.
Chicago, IL 60646

Pro-Life Action Ministries*
611 S. Snelling Ave.
St. Paul, MN 55116

Rutherford Institute*
P. O. Box 510
Manassas, VA 22110

Sex Respect*
P. O. Box 349
Bradley, IL 60915

Why Wait?*
P. O. Box 1000
Dallas, TX 75221

Women Exploited (WE)*
2100 W. Ainsley
Chicago, IL 60640

Women Exploited by Abortion
  (WEBA)*
202 S. Andrews
Three Rivers, MI 49093

Endnote

1. George Grant, *Grand Illusions* (Brentwood, Tennessee: Wolgemuth & Hyatt, 1988), pp. 295-297.

SUGGESTED READING

Andrews, Joan. *THE PRISON LETTERS OF JOAN ANDREWS*. Richard Cowden-Guido, ed. Brentwood, Tennessee: Wolgemuth & Hyatt, 1988.

Belz, Mark. *SUFFER THE LITTLE CHILDREN*. Westchester, Illinois: Crossway Books, A Division of Good News Publishers, 1989.

deParrie, Paul. *The Rescuers*. Brentwood, Tennessee: Wolgemuth & Hyatt, 1989.

Eidsmoe, John. *God and Caesar*. Westchester, Illinois: Crossway Books, A Division of Good News Publishers, 1984.

Fowler, Paul B. *Abortion: Toward an Evangelical Consensus*. Portland, Oregon: Multnomah Press, 1987.

Grant, George. *Grand Illusions*. Brentwood, Tennessee: Wolgemuth & Hyatt, 1988.

Nathanson, Bernard N., M.D., with Ostling, Richard N. *Aborting America*. Garden City, New York: Doubleday and Company, 1979.

Powell, John, S.J. *Abortion: The Silent Holocaust*. Valencia, California: Tabor Publishing Company, a division of DLM, Inc., 1981.

Reagan, Ronald. *Abortion and the Conscience of the Nation*. Nashville, Tennessee: Thomas Nelson, 1984.

Schaeffer, Franky. *A Time for Anger*. Westchester, Illinois: Crossway Books, A Division of Good News Publishers, 1982.

Schaeffer, Francis A. and Koop, C. Everett, M.D. *Whatever Happened to the Human Race?* Old Tappan, New Jersey: Fleming H. Revell, 1979.

Scheidler, Joseph M. *Closed: Ninety-Nine Ways To Stop Abortion.* San Francisco: Ignatius Press, 1985.

Smith, Donald S., Don Tanner, ed. *The Silent Scream.* Anaheim, California: American Portrait Films Books, 1985.

Terry, Randall. *Operation Rescue.* Springdale, Pennsylvania: Whitaker House, 1988.

BIBLIOGRAPHY

Andrews, Joan. Richard Cowden-Guido, Ed. *THE PRISON LETTERS OF JOAN ANDREWS*. Brentwood, Tennessee: Wolgemuth & Hyatt, Publishers, Inc., 1988.

Aurant, Paul. *Paul Harvey's The Rest of the Story*. New York: Bantam, 1977.

Belz, Mark. *SUFFER THE LITTLE CHILDREN*. Westchester, Illinois: Crossway Books, A Division of Good News Publishers, 1989.

Blake, Nelson Manfred. *A Short History of American Life*. New York: McGraw-Hill Book Company, Inc., 1952.

Bryce, Ron, M.D. "The Killing of a 'Nonperson.' " *Pentecostal Evangel*. June 11, 1989.

Feder, Don. "Sick of Death." *The Pentecostal Evangel*. November 27, 1988.

Fowler, Paul B. *Abortion: Toward an Evangelical Consensus*. Portland, Oregon: Multnomah, 1987.

Grant, George. *Grand Illusions*. Brentwood, Tennessee: Wolgemuth & Hyatt, 1988.

Horn, Carl. "How Freedom of Thought Is Smothered in America." *Christianity Today*. April 6, 1984.

Kass, Leon R. Dr. "Making Babies — The New Biology and the 'Old' Morality." *The Public Interest*. Winter 1972.

Marshall, Peter and Manuel, David. *The Light and the Glory*. Old Tappan, New Jersey: Fleming H. Revell, 1977.

"Memories of My Abortion," an article in the advertising supplement of an Oklahoma City newspaper, produced and paid for by Life Issues, Inc. January 1989.

Nathanson, Bernard N., M.D., with Ostling, Richard N. *Aborting America*. Garden City, New York: Doubleday and Company, 1979.

"Post-Abortion Syndrome," an article in the advertising supplement of an Oklahoma City newspaper, produced and paid for by Life Issues, Inc. January 1989.

Powell, John, S.J. *Abortion: The Silent Holocaust*. Valencia, California: Tabor Publishing Company, a division of DLM, Inc., 1981.

"PROCLAMATION 5761 OF JANUARY 14, 1985; NATIONAL SANCTITY OF HUMAN LIFE DAY, 1988." *Federal Register*. Vol. 53, No. 11. Tuesday, January 19, 1988.

Schaeffer, Francis A. and Koop, C. Everett, M.D. *Whatever Happened to the Human Race?* Old Tappan, New Jersey: Fleming H. Revell, 1979.

Smith, Donald S., Don Tanner, ed. *The Silent Scream*. Anaheim, California: American Portrait Films Books, 1985.

State of Florida v. Joan Elizabeth Andrews, in the Circuit Court in and for Escambia County, Florida, Case No. 86-1663-CFAS. September 25, 1986.

Terry, Randall. *Operation Rescue*. Springdale, Pennsylvania: Whitaker House, 1988.

The Wall Street Journal. July 5, 1989.

Richard Exley is an intense person who cares deeply for people which is reflected in both his writing and teaching. He is widely recognized for his daily radio broadcast "Straight From the Heart" which focuses on people rather than issues and is touching America with the love of God.

Richard Exley is the author of five books: *Blue-Collar Christianity, Perils of Power, The Rhythm of Life, The Other God — Seeing God as He Really Is,* and *The Painted Parable.* He currently pastors Christian Chapel in Tulsa, Oklahoma, where he lives with his wife, Brenda.

To contact Richard Exley, write:

Richard Exley
7807 E. 76th St.
Tulsa, OK 74133-3648

Other Honor Books by Richard Exley

Blue-Collar Christianity

Perils of Power

The Rhythm of Life

Available from your local bookstore
or by writing:

P. O. Box 55388
Tulsa, Oklahoma 74155

INFINITY

ABORTION:
Pro-Life by Conviction,
Pro-Choice by Default

NEW VIDEO!

RICHARD EXLEY

ABORTION:

Pro-Life by Conviction, Pro-Choice by Default

Taped live at the "Stop the American Holocaust"
Pro-Life rally in Tulsa, Oklahoma.
Only $19.95

Order yours from **INFINITY VIDEO** today!
Call TOLL-FREE 1-800-678-2126
or write
Infinity Video • P.O. Box 55388
Tulsa, Oklahoma 74155.

VRE-001/1995 ISBN 0-89274-701-3